Stuart Morris was born on Portland, and his roots on the Island go back many generations. His interest in Portland's history was fostered by the discovery of his family's involvement with quarrying, the Breakwater, fishing and even smuggling. For twelve years he represented Portland on the Dorset County Council, and was an ardent campaigner for the local environment. Since 1991 he has been Highways Agency Manager for the local borough council. He is the author of *Portland, An Illustrated History* (1985), *Portland Camera* (1990), and other local books.

Following page
Perhaps Portland's most famous view, but when this photograph was taken in about 1898 tourists could only reach the spot by foot or horse carriage. Below the boys lazing in the sunshine on the cliff edge at Priory is the ancient fishing village of Chiswell. Beyond and still in its natural state, is the tidal Mere, a notable wildlife habitat. Eight years later the first of the navy's huge fuel tanks were built adjacent to the beachside railway.

DISCOVER DORSET

PORTLAND

STUART MORRIS

THE DOVECOTE PRESS

Several fine masonry arches like this were built
to carry horse-drawn stone trucks over the network
of tracks and cuttings. The best surviving example
is Lano's Arch of 1854 in what is now
Tout Quarry Park.

First published in 1998 by The Dovecote Press Ltd
Stanbridge, Wimborne, Dorset BH21 4JD

ISBN 1 874336 49 0

Series designed by Humphrey Stone

Typeset in Sabon by The Typesetting Bureau
Wimborne, Dorset
Printed and bound by Baskerville Press, Salisbury, Wiltshire

A CIP catalogue record for this book is available
from the British Library

CONTENTS

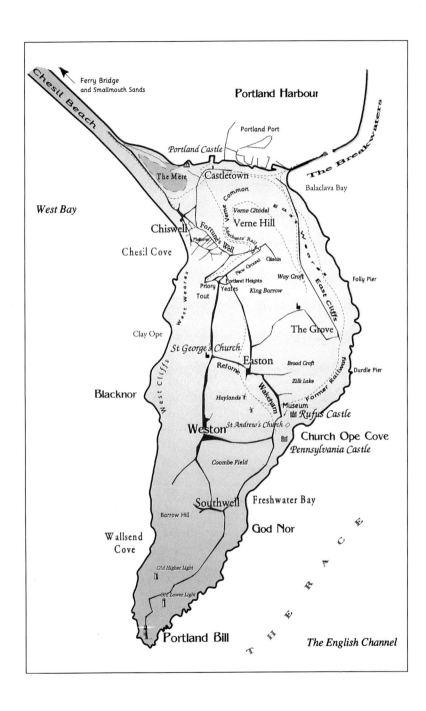

Ferry Bridge
and Smallmouth Sands

Portland Harbour

Portland Port

Portland Castle

The Mere   **Castletown**

Balaclava Bay

Common

West Bay

Verne Citadel

Verne Hill

Chiswell

Fortune's Well

Merchants' Rail

Chesil Cove

New Ground   *Chalets*

Portland Heights

Priory   Yeates   *King Barrow*

Tout

Way Croft

Folly Pier

Clay Ope

The Grove

St George's Church

Easton

Broad Croft

Durdle Pier

Reforne

Zilk Lake

Blacknor

Haylandɛ

Museum

Rufus Castle

Weston   *St Andrew's Church*

Church Ope Cove

Pennsylvania Castle

Coombe Field

Southwell   Freshwater Bay

Barrow Hill

God Nor

**W allsend
Cove**

Old Higher Light

Old Lower Light

Portland Bill

The English Channel

ISLAND OF DISCOVERY

The Island and Royal Manor of Portland is unique, and to this day remains one of the most striking and fascinating places in Britain. Such is its character and history, that wherever you go on the Island there is always more to discover. To describe Portland as an 'island' is perhaps misleading. Despite the name in reality it is a 4½-mile long and 1¾-mile wide peninsula of limestone anchored to Chesil Beach, the slender shingle arc which through millennia has retreated progressively across Lyme Bay.

Physically the Island is divided into two distinct parts. The escarpment facing Weymouth is a vast slope of ancient rock scree, curving in dramatic convex and concave land forms around Portland's summit, Verne Hill. This area, known as Underhill, is all that can be seen from the mainland. Closely packed buildings now spill down the steep valley from Tillycoombe through Fortune's Well to Chiswell, the southern termination of Chesil Beach.

Over the hill, a plateau – the greater part of the Island – descends gently southward towards the extremity of Portland Bill. Tophill is the surface of the geological strata containing the famous Portland Stone beds. The Portland Beds date from around 140 million years ago and are of marine origin, containing many fossils from a subtropical sea. This Jurassic limestone has for centuries provided one of the world's best building materials.

Portland has been occupied continuously since prehistoric times, and signs of those far-off people are still being discovered. Evidence of Middle Stone Age Portlanders has been found on south-facing slopes at Culverwell, near the Bill, and at other sites. The island's isolated position and narrow link with the mainland made those who lived on it a strong, self-sufficient community. Portlanders may have been insular, but they were proud and law abiding (locked doors and places of confinement were unknown until people from the

The Portland peninsula from the air. Chesil Beach is on the right, while to its leeward are the calm waters of the Fleet lagoon, separated from Portland Harbour by Ferry Bridge.

mainland began to settle here). A newspaper remarked in 1863, 'Portlanders are a fine, strong and healthy race, greatly superior in ordinary stature, both in person and intelligence. This is partly attributed to the fine air, and comparatively good living.'

UNDER THE HILL

UNDERHILL

The densely developed north-west slope of Verne Hill facing West Bay is known as Underhill. Picturing Underhill in ancient times we would see, below crude earth ramparts on the hilltop, a line of dwellings around a spring at Fortune's Well. The Romans knew this spot, and must have lived here for generations, for their relics have been unearthed and we know that they buried their dead in stone coffins further around the hillside. Many of these were found on Verne Common when the large housing estate covered the grassy slopes in the 1950's.

The summit of Verne Hill was an ancient beacon site, and later a semaphore signal station was placed there. The hill itself – the Great Common – was a vast open pasture, stretching from the Mere at Chiswell over the hilltop towards the Grove, and right down to the water's edge around the north-east side. Here residents had the historic right to freely roam and play, and to graze their sheep and cattle. The hill was the stage for Cow-common Day, held every May 14th from time out of mind. This was the day when the cattle were turned out on the Common for the summer. Dancing, music, garlands and games made this the merry highlight of the year for Portlanders, young and old. The custom died out in the mid-nineteenth century when the Government purchased the whole Common for defences.

CHISWELL

From Fortune's Well a stream ran down steep grassy banks, by the tiny hamlets of Mallams and Maiden Well, to Chiswell (once known as Chesilton), where cottages were built literally into the back slope of the beach.

The Mere was a wide tidal lagoon enclosed by two arms of shingle (Coneygar Bank) with a gap through which small craft could enter. Before the entire area was filled in, first for the fuel tanks (from 1906), later for the Royal Naval Air Station (from 1956), it was used for sheep washing. It teamed with wildfowl, for the saltwater creek of the Mere anciently extended far along what is now the main street of Chiswell, between the beach and a low cliff running from Clements Lane to Chesil Cove. The creek was gradually filled in and in time the village and its street straddled it, to become by the seventeenth century a well-populated, bustling village of fishermen, seafarers, and quarrymen.

The buildings of old Chiswell were constructed of large, thick

In the late nineteenth century Chiswell was a thriving community. The stout houses on the back of the shingle bank were built to withstand occasional flooding by storm waves. The twin gables at the far end of the village were on the 1865 railway terminus. To the right are the hillside hamlets of Mallams and Maidenwell, separated by well-tended gardens and closes.

The Cove House Inn has stood on the top of Chesil Beach, defying the sea, for 250 years. It was one of many houses robustly built on the beach, but many have been destroyed, not by the sea but by ill-judged clearance schemes. The fishing village of Chiswell has existed since well before the Middle Ages. Beyond are the neat walled fields of Killicks Hill and Lancridge (since built on), in contrast to the wild West Weares, extending to the right.

block stone walls, with thatched or stone slat roofs supported on stout timbers, often salvaged from shipwrecks. Access straight up to the beach and sea was through a series of narrow passages or 'opes' between the buildings. Beneath were cellars where smuggled goods could be hidden, and most houses had floodways to carry over-topping seawater safely down to the street. The Cove House Inn is typical of these, but since the early 1920's many of its compatriots have been lost.

The Cove House Inn commands a unique view of Chesil Cove and West Bay. Built right on the crest of the beach, nothing better symbolises the villagers' defiance of and kinship with the sea. Dating back to at least the mid-eighteenth century, the inn was an important meeting house for locals throughout its history. It was held in the same family for over 200 years, and it figured strongly in the saga of shipwrecks on this part of the coast, the record of which is among the most numerous and tragic in the British Isles. Watch was kept from its windows, survivors were taken in, and bodies of victims were taken to the nearby 'Dead House'. Among countless

Chiswell Square in 1928. Tiny Victorian shops mingle with old cottages along the wide street. On the skyline at Priory Corner is the crane used for loading stone onto the Merchants Railway. The natural cliff faces above are partly buried under two centuries of surplus rock tipped from the quarries.

such events, the Cove House Inn featured strongly in the infamous *Avalanche* and *Forest* disaster of 1877, when the landlady comforted the few survivors.

The most devastating event in Chiswell's history was the Great Gale of 1824, when 80 houses were destroyed, and 27 people lost their lives – the only recorded direct fatalities by sea flooding in this area. However, like the other robust buildings on the beach, the Cove House Inn survived this and countless other sea storms virtually unscathed. Most were built to withstand everything the sea could throw at them, like the nearby New Hotel, where a storm in 1853 pitched a fishing boat onto the roof! The New Hotel was a favourite with eighteenth century visitors, and in the 1820s Island Governor John Penn held public balls there, entertaining titled gentry. This place, like the Crown Inn and too many other Georgian,

Tudor, and older buildings in Chiswell, was needlessly demolished in the twentieth century, not by the sea, but by official decree, for want of imagination and confidence. However much remains of the rich character of this ancient fishing village, which is now well protected against sea flooding by a fine sea wall promenade, and by massive barriers and culverts buried within the beach. As the twentieth century closes, restoration and new building is invigorating this true maritime community.

At the entrance to Chiswell, Victoria Square, as its name suggests, was formed in the mid-nineteenth century. It was the vision of one man, Captain Charles Manning of Portland Castle. He bought the old Poor House there, and some land from the Crown, to build elegant terraces, and also the striking Victoria Lodge Hotel. On the Weymouth side of the Square stood the charming Portland Railway Station (built 1864, demolished 1969). The utilitarian Portland Gas Works (1865-1959) was here as well, but even that had superb ashlar walling and a carved stone archway: a rather incongruous plant hire yard now occupies the site. Years of decline were strikingly reversed when Victoria Square was enhanced with flower beds, paving and ornamental lighting, featuring a large anchor from Portland Harbour. HRH The Duke of York marked the completion of this regeneration scheme in 1996 by unveiling a commemorative stone there.

FORTUNE'S WELL

Overlooking Chiswell a series of springs served Maidenwell, the incredibly steep Mallams, and Fortune's Well (the fresh water still runs but is now piped underground). Here can be found two of the island's grandest surviving houses, of about 1750. Both Queen Anne House at the top of Fortune's Well, and Claremont at Maidenwell, were built by wealthy quarry agents. Queen Anne House is one of the finest small town houses of its period, while Claremont was for 100 years of its existence a ruined shell, around which abounded as many romantic legends as there were stones in its classic walls. Yet many generations of families resided there before its decay. This small mansion was brilliantly restored to its original palladian-style glory in 1997.

These are not the oldest buildings in Underhill. Among other fine buildings is the Portland Arms Inn, where the arms and uniforms of the Portland Militia were kept in the 1750's. Here George III relished the landlady's special 'Royal Puddings' on his many visits to Portland at the turn of the nineteenth century. There are several truly ancient cottages, some much altered over centuries, which nestle beside Victorian and later edifices.

The steep hillside of Fortune's Well has always called for special measures. St John's Church (1839) had to be built in line with the contours, not the normal east-west orientation. One side of the narrow main street is supported on unseen eighteenth/nineteenth century retaining walls running its entire length, from Queens Road to New Road. The other side of the road is cut unto the ground.

Were it not for the thousands of engineers, staff and workers attracted here in a mad late nineteenth century rush due to the great Portland Harbour and Verne works, the entire Underhill area would have taken on a totally different character. Until then many stone merchants, traders and sea captains chose to live here in neat dwellings, no doubt enjoying the tang of the sea and the spectacular views. It was also more convenient than Tophill for access to the mainland by land or sea. Their extensive walled gardens were planted, not only for produce, but for ornament. But when the government works started everything changed. Many farm closes and green spaces were hastily built upon to house the new arrivals. Terrace upon steep terrace extended up the hillside, some even in red brick – quite alien to this 'Island of Stone'. These sinuous rows of slated roofs now dominate the character of Underhill, which retains great charm for all that.

Opposite page Queen Anne House, Fortune's Well, is an architectural gem. It stands as a reminder of the way Underhill developed during the seventeenth and eighteenth centuries, before the Victorian Breakwater works caused smaller artisans houses to spring up in the hillside gardens. Queen Anne House was built in about 1750 by local quarry agent and architect Thomas Gilbert.
Opposite page bottom The centre pair of these charming eighteenth century cottages at Maidenwell was originally a single house of some importance. Its stone-mullioned windows were altered when converted in the nineteenth century.

This perfectly proportioned Wesleyan Chapel at Fortune's Well was erected in 1792 at the expense of wealthy Methodist Robert Carr Brackenbury.

Much more elegant were Underhill's fine Methodist chapels, and the impressive shops, banks, hotels and post office which Victorian entrepreneurs built with the prosperity brought by the Breakwater and Verne schemes. Tall, richly carved stone façades lined the narrow Fortune's Well street, in contrast to the earlier simpler dwellings. This became the business centre of Portland, and remained as such until well into the 1970s. Fortune's Well survived severe bomb damage in the Second World War, but many four-storey shop premises in the upper part of the street were lost. By the late twentieth century the rumble of motor traffic funnelling through the main street only a few paces wide had caused the demise of many well-established businesses. However, a widespread refurbishment scheme launched in 1995 has already brought new life and confidence to Underhill, where many Kimberlins (people from the mainland) are again taking up residence alongside settled Portlanders.

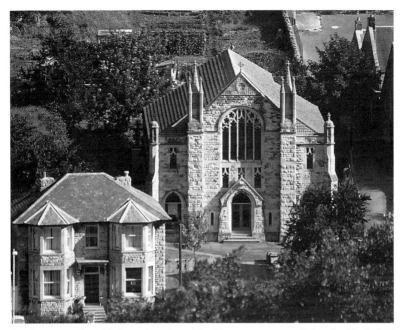

By the 1890s the old Georgian chapel had become too small for the Underhill congregation. An architectural competition resulted in the superb pinnacled façade of Brackenbury Memorial Church which opened in 1900.

CASTLETOWN

Castletown grew in the lee of the Portland Castle, which gave it its name. It was unlike other parts of the Island; being remote from the quarries and the farms it did not develop as a village settlement, and it only ever boasted one short street of houses along the water front. However, fishermen and bathers used the long beach between the Castle and Portland Nor, where in the 1790s thriving shipbuilding yards launched smacks, brigs and cutters. A number of sheerleg cranes and derricks clustered around the small stone quay, and the Old Castle Hotel had a steady trade from men-o'-war and merchant ships taking refuge in the Roadstead. The new stone pier constructed to serve the Merchant's Railway (1826) brought more activity, but the character of Castletown changed beyond recognition when the Breakwater works started. By the 1860's they were Dorset's major tourist attraction. The pier was enlarged to take regular paddle steamers from Weymouth. Hotels, pubs, shops and a barber opened along the waterfront to serve the thousands of sailors and civilian personnel. Right up to the 1990's Castletown's hotels and pubs – the Portland Roads, Royal Breakwater, Jolly Sailor, The Albert and Sailors' Return – filled to overflowing whenever the Fleet was in.

In the Second World War Castletown was virtually closed to civilians when it became the centre of a great embarkation of Allied

Edwardian Castletown catered to sailors every needs. There was a grocer, barber, coffee bar, reading room, chandlers, post office – and several large public houses.

Castletown Beach, the most sheltered on the Island, was gradually
encroached upon, first by the Stone Pier, seen here in 1900,
and by expanding naval developments.

troops for D-Day. But even after the War, as the gateway to the
Naval base, it remained in danger of being engulfed by naval activity.
In 1985 it was dwarfed by Portland's largest building project since
the construction of the Breakwater and Verne. Looming over the old
waterside street, this enormous £25 million development provided
accommodation for officers and ratings, and a superb swimming
sports centre. Little did anyone realise that with the ending of the
Cold War this would all be redundant within fifteen years, when
the navy left Portland. Happily, the vacuum did not last long, as
Castletown is now becoming a major centre for diving and other
water sports, as well as serving Portland Harbour's new commercial
maritime industries.

ON TOPHILL

Even on foot it was never easy to get over the great escarpment separating Underhill from Tophill. Two precipitous tracks, known as Old Hill and Verne Road, were originally only cartways. In 1810 William Moore and his son were contracted by quarry masters to construct a new road from the top at Priory near the edge of West Cliff to Fortune's Well. 'New Road' was a great improvement for normal traffic, and once a bridge to the mainland had been built in 1839, gave Tophill folk less excuse not to 'visit England', which many generations of Portlanders neither needed nor desired to do! New Road, reconstructed in the 1960s, now carries traffic undreamt

New Road (seen here in 1937) climbs up to Priory Corner. In 1996 the top section had to be diverted into a new deep cutting, away from the unstable cliff edge. In the centre the even steeper Old Hill, now just a footpath, can be seen skirting the eighteenth century rectory.

The entire hilltop ridge, from Verne Hill to West Cliff, commands a glorious view out over Fortune's Well and Chesil Beach.

of in William Moore's day, when the only link to the rest of Dorset was the ferry at Smallmouth.

By the 1980s New Road's future was in some doubt. The top of the road at Priory Corner was resting precariously on an old stone tip, which lay beyond the natural cliff-edge, and made the section unstable. A spectacular £1m scheme to divert the road in a deep cutting away from the cliff was finally completed in 1996, securing Tophill's only practicable road link. An old quarry derrick was restored and placed near the site of the original Priory crane on the Merchants' Railway. The new cutting caused the loss of the famous view from the road over Chesil, which visitors now have to leave their cars to enjoy.

On the hill, in the area now sometimes called Portland Heights, are (east to west) Glacis, New Ground, Yeates, Priory and Tout. The names give clues to the story of these parts. 'Glacis' is actually a military term for open ground deliberately created to provide a clear line of fire from a fortress, in this case Verne Citadel. The edge of the entire escarpment from the Verne to West Cliff was quarried in the 1700s and early 1800's, and was restored by convict labour in the late nineteenth century. New Ground was just that, being levelled in the 1880's, and used as a parade and sports ground. Today it is a tourists vantage point for the famous birds' eye view along Chesil Beach.

The Portland Heights Hotel building at Yeates was started as a one man enterprise in 1969 on the site of a car park and wooden cafe. It has grown into one of the most celebrated hotels in Weymouth and Portland, with one of the best views in England. Its enormously deep foundations descend into a filled quarry far beneath it, in which are buried railway cuttings, tunnels and stables – all of which could still be seen until the 1950's.

'Yeates' (from the Old English meaning gap), takes its name from a deep natural crevasse which once existed between Verne Hill and the land to the south. Cartloads of prehistoric bones and fossils were found in this chasm when it was gouged out for the great Verne Ditch works from 1870. 'Priory' is more obscure; the name probably dates from the twelfth century when the Priory of St Swithin, Winchester, held the Manor of Portland, while 'tout' is an Old English term for look-out.

The name Tout is as old as the small clifftop fields and paddocks which were here long before Jonathan Lano and others quarried the land and built small tunnels and bridges in the nineteenth century. The spot has unrivalled panoramic views along Chesil Beach, and was a vital defensive vantage point through the centuries. Now designated 'Tout Quarry Park' this incredible area is a maze of craggy cuttings where Nature is regaining her ground, but around every corner can be discovered the work of visiting sculptors – rocks and cliff faces imaginatively carved into beautiful and weird forms. It has become a mecca for lovers of the Portland spirit, and has already featured in countless TV programmes and magazines.

Opposite page top Old bridge in Inmosthay.
Opposite page bottom Tout Quarry Park. The sheltered cuttings of the old quarry are now a popular sculpture park.

The pattern of fields and settlements on this part of the Island was established more than a thousand years ago. Eight great open fields were divided into broad strips called 'furlongs' – the length of a furrow. These in turn were partitioned into a total of some 2,400 strip fields in classic medieval arrangement. Dividing the fields were dry walls of slatt stone, and baulks of earth called lynchets. Some of these ancient strip fields can still be seen, mainly beyond Southwell towards Portland Bill. Sadly however, the vast majority – despite having survived unscathed for the last millennium – have gradually been destroyed by quarrying and housing.

It is hard to find any undisturbed land between Portland Heights and the main Tophill settlement, Easton. Here amid old and current quarries, are now hi-tech industrial units, Chesil Beach Motors, stone masonry works – and a delightful network of footpaths. Yet these quarry grounds are not ancient by Portland standards, for until the 1840's this was a completely pastoral landscape.

The land right across the Island between the quarries at East and West Cliffs was once a scene of sheep and cattle grazing, horse-ploughs and of women working – the fields were worked mainly by the women, their menfolk being fishermen, quarrymen, or both. Here also was a great prehistoric burial mound – King Barrow – and by Easton Lane a group of mysterious standing stones known as the Frolic. These are gone, and are now only survived by a small fragment of a 'fossil forest', which excited tourists when the ground was being stripped in the 1850's.

Perhaps the most astounding features ever found on Tophill were sets of underground 'dene hole' chambers. The purpose of these large conical stone structures, which contained animal bones, grain and sling stones and were constructed by prehistoric Portlanders, remains a mystery, but several groups were unearthed at King Barrow, Coombe Field and Broad Croft near Wakeham. Had all these features been found in the twentieth century, instead of in less enlightened times, they would have attracted national interest,

Until the mid nineteenth century the entire Tophill landscape was a patchwork of small strip fields, separated by earthen lynchets, or dry stone walls. Most have vanished, destroyed by quarrying or housing estates. Those that remain – as here near Portland Bill – are a rare legacy of a historic farming pattern.

although what priceless artefacts have been gobbled up unseen by modern quarry excavators we shall never know. King Barrow and other fields between the Verne and the Grove, and the land across the top of Yeates to Priory, were acquired in the 1860's by the Admiralty for convicts to quarry.

Fascination also lies in the disused stone bridges and the network of intricate cuttings of Tout, Waycroft and Kingbarrow, now supremely enriched by the flora and fauna that make much of Portland's natural history both rare and nationally important. As well as a profusion of wild flowers, the limestone is home to many lichens and several rare mosses. The old quarries have been colonised by a unique form of the silver-studded blue butterfly. The Portland ribbon

wave moth lives in the rough grassland near the cliff, whilst another rare moth is only found at one other site in the country.

The Tophill 'hamlets' of Easton, Weston, Reforne Wakeham and Southwell were at the focal points of the great open fields, where there were natural springs and watercourses. Surrounding each of the fields were the common pastures, broad green belts which stretched between the settlements. Although Portland cannot be described as well-wooded, and few trees are to be found on the more open ground, there have always been ample trees around Wakeham and the other villages, and increasingly in the old quarry workings. The open fields were where the 'tenants of the Manor' enjoyed the full range of ancient common rights, which they exercised for countless centuries. Portland's commons, which also include pockets of land on the cliffs and undercliffs, Portland Bill and much of Chesil Beach, are still carefully guarded by the ancient Court Leet, which today is almost unique in that it still retains some legal powers.

EASTON AND REFORNE

The most prominent of Portland's historic buildings is St George's Church at Reforne. Before this the Island's main meeting place, the old St Andrew's at Church Ope Cove, was by the 1750s in danger of falling over the cliff. Local architect and builder Thomas Gilbert produced superb plans for a new church in a more central location. His design was undoubtedly influenced by the work of Sir Christopher Wren, for whom Gilbert's grandfather had been quarry agent seventy years earlier. The church was financed by the Portland Stone Grant Fund, a Parish rate, a donation from George II, and even by the freehold sale of pew sittings. Owners were required to keep their pews in good repair, which was fine when all owners were known and close at hand, but impossible to enforce as years went on and families became dispersed.

Some of the Island's best stonemasons and craftsmen spent twelve

The many public footpaths through the old quarries give the opportunity to discover not only Portland's industrial archaeology, but its geology and rich natural history.

years building the new church. Finally, in July 1776, Dr Newton, Bishop of Bristol, arrived to consecrate St George's Church, having first been carried shoulder high over the water at Smallmouth. A year later a house was built just across the road in Reforne for the parish clerk, William Butts. Conveniently, the new house stood next door to the George Inn, one of the Island's oldest and best loved hostelries, allowing William Butts to combine his spiritual duties with more worldly pleasures.

St George's served the Island well for 150 years, but as time went on congregations tired of the stiff backs caused by the narrow hardback pews and draughty unheated conditions. Worse, the pews were private freehold property, which absent owners often held for their exclusive use – so the church was poorly attended. This deliberate neglect is our reward, for the Victorians did not 'modernize' it – as they did with so many churches elsewhere in Dorset – and visitors are able to admire its fine original Georgian features. Although officially redundant, St George's Church is now under the care of the Churches Conservation Trust, and is enthusiastically looked after by a group of volunteer Friends. It is now deservedly regarded as one of the most interesting and unspoilt examples of Georgian architecture in the county.

St George's was eventually replaced by the light and lofty All Saints' Church, set amongst trees just off Easton Square, and which remains one of the few public buildings anywhere in England to be completed during the First World War.

For centuries the Great Pool dominated the centre of Easton, which is in a natural hollow in the landscape. It was once, no doubt, a charming village pond, surrounded by wide greens and a square of simple cottages. However, four roads converged here, and as the population increased carts churned up the ground, and the large pond became muddy and unusable. For drinking and washing water a 35 metre-deep well was sunk nearby in 1775, and the old Pool was finally was filled in around 1885, depriving the Punchbowl Inn of its source of water for brewing!

Easton Square has witnessed many of the most important events in Portland's history. It was here that in 1803 Portlanders fought off a naval press gang of twenty-nine men, armed with muskets, bayonets,

St George's Church, Reforne, is a gloriously unspoilt example of Georgian architecture. Although superseded by All Saints Church in 1917, it is now cared for by local volunteers and the Churches Conservation Trust. Its graveyard memorials are among the best of their era.

Children pose in their Sunday best by the new bandstand in Easton Gardens in 1906. To the right of the ornate bandstand a stone clock tower was added a year later.

pistols and cutlasses, in a notorious episode now known as the Easton Massacre. In the struggle three men and a girl were shot dead. A Royal Charter of 1453 had freed Portlanders for ever from Admiralty jurisdiction, and the Islanders knew that the navy had no right impress men on the Island.

In 1902 an inspired decision was made to turn the barren wilderness of Easton Square into public gardens. The transformation of the Square into elegant Edwardian flower-beds and walks was remarkable. A magical sight greeted the hundreds of people who came to see Easton Gardens opened in the summer of 1904. In place of the Great Pool and the revered old Easton pump, a low wall and railings enclosed lawns, exotic trees, shrubs and a fine bandstand. Three years later a stone clock tower with four illuminated faces was unveiled, the only timepiece many people saw in their working day.

On each side of the Square impressive buildings appeared; to the south, the Jubilee Hall of 1888 (now the South Portland Working

Men's Conservative Club); to the north, a fine residence, 'Nether-coombe', for quarry owner Henry Sansom (1901); to the east, Pearce's drapery store with pinnacled turret (now the Co-op). The crowning glory was the Easton Wesleyan Church which was completed in 1907, by the same builder who had just erected the new lighthouse. The twin-spired building displays some of the finest examples of the masons' craft to be seen on Portland. Below the pulpit is a relief of Leonardo de Vinci's 'Last Supper', exquisitely carved from a single block of whitbed stone hewn from Headland quarry at The Grove.

The public library in Straits is on the site of the Island's first school, This simple low 'Maister's School' was established near the heart of Easton in about 1720. It was Portland's only free day school for more than a hundred years, until 1857, when two magnificent new schools were built – St John's, Fortune's Well, and St George's, Reforne. These were funded by compensation paid by the government to the Islanders for the loss of their Great Common for the Verne and Breakwater schemes. Both buildings had south-facing archways, and were impressively large and well-equipped. The school at Underhill was bombed (without casualties) in 1940, and the last pupils left St George's in 1969 – since when it has been beautifully restored as St George's Community Centre.

1997 saw the completion of a superb YMCA centre, almost next door, which is carefully crafted in Portland Stone to complement the style of the Victorian school. Ironically, this too was one of many projects part-funded by government money, a regeneration grant effectively given to compensate the Island for the loss of its Naval Base.

The castellated building on Easton Lane, leading from Portland Heights, is the Drill Hall of 1868. It was once the home of the Portland Volunteers, who were originally formed to man the new gun emplacements. Further down the road at Grove Corner a terrace of cottages now stands on the site of the historic Crown Farm, the demesne farm of the Royal Manor. It was bombed in 1942, but after the war much of the Crown's farmland in this part of the Island was quarried or built on anyway.

The roads of Tophill are as broad as Underhill's are narrow. Each of Tophill's villages has a distinctive character. Wakeham may be the oldest, and was once the most populous part of the Island. In Saxon times the houses extended down the dell to the clifftop above Church Ope. Wells and objects found there from this period show that the original village probably centred in the miniature valley, whose small watercourse flowed through what are now the grounds of Pennsylvania Castle.

Pennsylvania Castle holds pride of place on the Island. It was built for John Penn, the last Governor of Portland, son of George III's lady-in-waiting, and grandson of the founder of Pennsylvania USA. Having accompanied the king on excursions around the Island in the late 1790's, Penn was enchanted by Church Ope Cove. The celebrated architect James Wyatt perfectly placed the new maritime mansion he designed for Penn on a delightful natural platform high above the beach and elm-covered dell. From here Portland's Governor could enjoy breathtaking views of the English Channel beyond the Cove. The king provided the land, and his daughter Princess

A nineteenth century engraving of Rufus Castle and Pennsylvania Castle.

Cottages at Wakeham: simple porches, solid stone walls, and long gardens.

Elizabeth performed the opening ceremony in 1800. It was converted to a hotel in 1950, but in 1995 was lavishly restored to its former opulence as a private residence. Previous governors are believed to have lived in a large Tudor house near the top of Wakeham. It was known as Girt House, and though it may have been built in the 1500s by a wealthy stone merchant it has long since disappeared. Only a few of its features can still be seen, absorbed into later cottages on the west side of the street. The buildings fronting the extremely wide road of Wakeham are almost timeless. Some are easy to date, like the cottage Bartholemew Mitchell built in 1640 – he had the date and his initials carved into the gable. This is now the marvellous Portland Museum, whose displays and handful of rooms superbly capture the flavour of the Island's rich past. Many of Wakeham's lovingly restored cottages actually have origins far older even than hinted at by the traces of stone mullioned windows and rustic porchways. Successive generations of occupants altered and updated the simple dwellings with stone near at hand, to the style of their day. But the foundations and basic blocks may have been laid hundreds of years earlier.

The charming old Weston Pond as it looked in 1890. The pond has since been filled in and grassed over. A stone culvert carried water to it from Merry Well at the top end of the village, near Pound Piece.

WESTON

Until quite recently, Weston and Southwell were rural villages, quiet and almost untouched by the great upheavals which so changed the other settlements over 150 years. In the 1780s Weston had only 86 residents living in 15 houses. It had a pond at each end of the village, fed by a tiny stream which flowed from Merry Well, near Pound Piece. The delightful pond near Weston Corner was surrounded by huge boulders, with a few steps for access for washing and water-collecting. It was filled in around 1903 after Portland's first piped water supply was laid from Upwey .

Through Weston's wide open greens, cattle were driven and sheep gathered, and there was still ample room for the horse-drawn stone trucks to pass. Many a country village would be envious of the size of Weston's greens, where countless fêtes have been held. The tradition is continued today with the annual Gooseberry Fayre (after Bob 'Gooseberry' Comben, a one-time local postmaster). Weston had no church of its own, but in 1858 and 1860 villagers built for themselves two Methodist chapels.

On the west side of the road, tucked behind some early Victorian cottages is a remarkable sixteenth century house, actually a wing of a large detached residence which was partly demolished in the early nineteenth century. This was a dwelling of some importance, and although it lay in ruins for more than 120 years its many Tudor features were still intact when it was faithfully restored in 1991.

Opposite, and also partly hidden, is Gypsy Lane, where a charming thatched cottage can be found. Its identical partner was pulled down in around 1895, but it is a priceless survivor of the type of house which once existed all over the Island. The attraction of Weston, like much of Portland, is the random mixture of architectural styles. Other historic buildings still fronting the greens include the village farmhouse (No.83), and Weston House, a huge Edwardian home

This delightful Tudor cottage, modestly sited in Gypsy Lane off Weston Green, is lucky to have survived early twentieth century demolition schemes: its identical neighbour was not so lucky.

Relics of Portland's agrarian past, these ancient windmills were busy right up to the end of the nineteenth century. The stone towers still exist, on a hill between Wakeham and Weston. The watercolour is by Keith Lock of Southwell.

which originally had a rooftop platform from where the owner could survey his fields spreading away to the cliffs.

On the hill between Weston and Wakeham are the stone towers of the Island's two windmills, at Cottonfields and Growlands. Prominent landmarks for mariners, these were first recorded in the Land Revenue Accounts of 1608, but may have been built 100 years earlier. Grist was taken to the windmills for grinding from all over Tophill. They turned for the last time in the 1890s, but did not stop for want of wind!

Straying sheep were taken to the Court Leet's stone-walled cattle pound at Weston Road. This was rebuilt on the roadside green in 1950 to make way for a new estate of 100 houses – Pound Piece. The 1970s saw new estates expanding from old Weston towards the cliffs at Blacknor, and obliterating the lovely cornfields at Haylands. Then followed Weston's most fruitful development, the Royal Manor School, a focus for the energy and talents of future generations of Islanders.

'Up over Slobs, Down over Nobs, Dru the gate, and you be ther' was the way to Southwell. Time passed slowly in Dorset's most southerly village. So pure was the rich Portland dialect, that locals said the Saxons could have understood them. The soil around the village was rich and productive – the best strawberries in the county – and the mild climate ensured crops well ahead of the mainland.

Southwell is set in a shallow valley sheltered by low hills on three sides. It grew around a small stream running down between Bown Hill and Sweet Hill, along the street, and down over the cliff into Freshwater Bay. The village pond (which gave Southwell the nick-name Ducktown), was under what is now a children's playground near Avalanche Church. The stream runs through a culvert, but the last of the generation who could remember Portland's ponds before they were filled in passed away not long ago. Happily, many old buildings remain to give a flavour of what the village was once like. Cottages which once had stone-mullioned windows and slatstone or thatch roofs still exist in changed form, but the farmyard, which gave the centre of the village a real country atmosphere, has now closed.

Southwell had its own simple Methodist chapel tucked amongst the terraced cottages, with its back to the sea, but this closed in 1997 after serving the community well for 148 years. In contrast, the church standing on a knoll above the village owes its name to one of the most tragic episodes in the storm-tossed waters off Portland's coast. The *Avalanche* church was built to commemorate the collision of the three-masted clipper *Avalanche* and sailing ship *Forest* in 1877. The *Avalanche* was outward bound for New Zealand with sixty-three emigrants and returning families on board when on a September night it was struck amidships by the *Forest*. Four minutes later it had sunk. Most of the passengers were drowned in their beds, and its only survivors were twelve members of the ships' crews.

Such was the public horror a national fund was launched to build a memorial church on a site overlooking the scene of the collision. The Avalanche Memorial Church was consecrated two years later, remaining a permanent memorial to the 106 women, men and children who lost their lives that night. No longer could Islanders go 'up over Slobs', for in the wake of the disaster its name was changed to Avalanche Road.

A military camp was set up on Barrow Hill overlooking Southwell during the Second World War, when understandably little thought was given to tracing the ancient burial mound there. After the war, in 1949, work started on the largest building to be erected on Portland since the Verne Citadel. It began life as the Admiralty Gunnery Establishment, ending its days almost fifty years later as the Defence Research Establishment. At its peak 3000 scientists and administrators worked on the site, making it a larger employer than even the stone industry. In 1961 it was the setting for a classic spy case, featuring microdots, secret maps, dead-letter boxes and documents passed to Russian agents. The Old Bailey case against Harry Houghton and Ethel Gee shook the whole of the NATO alliance, and the full extent of the Soviet spy network was revealed only years later. But the Admiralty have now departed, and this superb clifftop site is now the Southwell Business Park.

Until 1965 Southwell was still a small village, but pressure for housing development was growing. Conservationists protested against 'cliff-to-cliff suburbia', pleading in vain for a cottage-style development with greens and open spaces. Gradually the pastoral landscape of Bown Hill disappeared for ever under the dense Sweethill housing estate, whose brick-built houses owe nothing to the original stonework in the old village.

Southwell is Dorset's most southerly village. This pastoral scene looking back from the Bill Road was the work of Swiss artist Samuel Grimm in 1790.

PORTLAND BILL

Beyond Southwell the scenery changes. The long single road meanders towards the Bill through an open landscape unchanged for centuries. The fields are still bordered with old walls and earth lynchets, although many strips were merged to increase production during the last war. Every field has a name, often of ancient obscurity, such as Harplands, Shoals Meadow, Sturt Corner, Dowerswell, Twin Croft, Rushetts, Lovers Line, and even a meadow called Scotland.

This is the only part of the Island's coast where the limestone cliffs rise directly from the sea. Erosion and weathering have produced some remarkable landforms – coves, ledges, undercuts, and caves, as well as the Blow Hole, which in storms produces spectacular water spouts. Viewing these low cliffs from seaward, a traveller in 1635 described them as resembling gates or portals, as if they were 'cut out by art' rather than nature. They certainly make an impressive – and in rough seas, awesome – coastline. Yet, from here on a clear, dead still night, it is sometimes possible to see the starlight reflected in the water.

Some of the cliffs around the Bill were quarried during the nineteenth century, in the course of which a great natural arch of rock (White Hole) was partially removed, leaving a stack which became well-known as 'Pulpit Rock'. Still to be found are remains of short tramways, which ran between the low quarry faces and loading derricks. The cranes there now are the only means of launching fishing boats. Unfortunately the quarrymen left piles of stone blocks covering several of the pebble beaches in the tiny coves. Yet, in summer these coves, with their rock-pools and cascading ledges are enjoyed by paddlers and bathers of all ages.

The famous Portland Bill lighthouse was fully automated in 1996, ending 280 years of continuous lighthouse keepers' duty. In early times occasional beacons and fires were lit on Branscombe Hill, the highest point near the Bill. The first lighthouses – a short one on the hill, a tall one nearer the coast – were erected in 1716 by private enterprise. As a pair, they aided navigation past the rocks and the treacherous tidal race, by day as well as night. Coal fires were lit behind glazed lanterns on the towers, but they were not very effective and did little to stem the number of shipwrecks around Portland's coast. Having originally opposed any lighthouse here, Trinity House eventually took over responsibility for the lights.

Newly invented oil lamps were installed when the Higher Lighthouse was rebuilt in 1788. The Lower Light was replaced a year later, and atop its incredible gothic style tower was an array of powerful oil lamps behind glass lenses. It was the first lighthouse in the world to use magnifying lenses, and such was their strength that the beam was visible at the horizon.

In spite of modernisation in the nineteenth century, and the erection of a high obelisk on the cliff edge, boldly inscribed 'T.H.1844' (Trinity House), technology moved on. The loss of some 14 ships near Portland in a terrible storm of 1901 led Trinity House to build a totally new lighthouse on the Bill. Foundations were dug deep into the rock, and the stone was quarried almost on the spot. After two years work in this exposed location the new Lighthouse was completed and lit for the first time on January 11th 1906. The revolving lenses floating on a bath of mercury sent a half-million candle-power beam (from a vaporised oil burner) 18 miles on a clear night. The bright red and white livery of Portland Bill Lighthouse has been Portland's most enduring symbol ever since.

The old lighthouses were eventually sold. The old Lower Lighthouse became the Portland Bird Observatory and Field Centre in 1961, and no place enjoys a better panorama of the English Channel than the fine residence converted from the old Higher Light on Branscombe Hill. Before 1922 there was only a rough cart track to the Bill, but once a proper road was built this formerly isolated part of the Island soon became one of Portland's main attractions. Cafes were opened, and no charabanc visit to Dorset was complete without a trip to the Bill, which has been firmly on the tourist map ever since. In the 1920s the old Higher Lighthouse was occupied by Dr Marie

Waves breaking over the old stone-loading derricks near Portland Bill
during a winter storm.

Stopes, the controversial pioneer of birth control, who in time became
a benefactor to Portland. From her hilltop retreat she witnessed with
dismay the gradual destruction of the orchid-strewn grass and the
solitude of Bill Point diminish as its popularity grew. By the 1930s 400
cars a day were visiting the new Portland Bill car park, and little
pleasure huts were mushrooming in nearby fields.

Today, even in the depth of winter, people drive for miles to watch
the spectacular storms that lash the Bill, afterwards taking refuge
in the The Pulpit Inn (1951). The former keepers' quarters of the
current Lighthouse are now a Tourist Information Centre.

THE STONE INDUSTRY

Portland Stone was being worked and exported from the Island in Roman times. The evidence lies in hundreds of their solid stone sarcophagi burials, and in Roman villas at Dorchester. To work the stone, the Romano-British Portlanders developed the skills of quarrying, cutting, and moving the huge blocks. Naturally exposed on the cliff faces, stone was broken off, squared, and, if not to be used locally, tumbled down to the foreshore for loading on to barges or rafts: until the Ferry Bridge was built in 1839 the only practicable route for exporting stone was by sea.

Following the Norman Conquest of 1066, William the Conqueror retained the strategically important Manor of Portland for himself. By then the qualities of its building stone were well-known, leading to its use by the Conqueror in parts of the Tower of London. By the fourteenth century Portland stone was being widely exported for domestic and public use. The quarries expanded and shipments went to Exeter Cathedral, Christchurch Priory, the Royal Palace at Westminster, and the original stone version of London Bridge.

On Portland itself, stone had already been beautifully worked for the Island's first proper church, the thirteenth century St Andrew's above Church Ope Cove. Above the church on a high rocky outcrop a clifftop defence was built in about 1400 to protect the landing place in the cove. It became known as 'Rufus' Castle, and was a model of the stonemason's craft. Hewn from nearby cliffs, the stone for it was accurately shaped and the mortar joints were as fine as could be achieved with the tools available. The seaward wall of the castle was built directly over a sheer cliff face, and the castle precinct extended inland. Looking at the ruins today, it is easy to visualise the form of both the church and the castle when they were the crux of Island activity.

Nowhere was the maturity of Portland's medieval stone industry

The ruins of the medieval St Andrew's Church, with the remains of Rufus (or Bow and Arrow) in the background. The two buildings were once the most important on the Island.

shown better than in the building known as The Vicar's House, of about 1300. This magnificent church-like chantry, which stood opposite the present Portland Museum at Wakeham, was the official residence of the first 25 or so rectors of the Island. Both the building and its contents, which included a library of rare books, were destroyed by Oliver Cromwell's troops in the Civil War, but its romantic ruins remained, in a beautiful wooded setting, until finally quarried away in 1917.

The prosperity brought to Portland by the stone industry in the early Middle Ages did not last. The Black Death decimated the population, which in turn was followed by the Hundred Years War with France. The Island bore the brunt of numerous ferocious raids, with the result that quarrying almost petered out. It took 200 years for the industry to recover, but the essential skills were never lost and it finally came back into fashion in the seventeenth century when Inigo Jones' Banqueting House at Whitehall (1622) proved the perfect advertisement for Portland Stone. Since then its reputation as the ideal building material for the nation's capital has rarely been disputed.

By its nature the Island coast was always subject to landslips. Quarrying activity in the cliffs upset the natural processes, and falls often coincided with peak stone production. They were of mixed blessing. On the one hand they exposed wide faces of fresh stone; on the other they destroyed the vital roads, and even the piers on the water's edge. To get to the valuable stone beds deep layers of over-burden had to be cleared away. This has always been a problem, even today, as can be seen by the huge temporary rubble banks in parts of Tophill. Quarrymen could tell the quality of stone partly by the note it made from a blow of the kivel, a short, heavy pick-shaped tool used to dress the stone. Another traditional Portland tool was the quarry jack, a simple but powerful mechanism capable of raising immense loads. Once quarried, the blocks were then roughly squared, carefully measured, marked, and either dragged on sleds or lifted onto carts to be taken to one of several piers, mainly along the Island's east coast.

Stone was quarried all around the edges of the Tophill plateau, including the escarpment at Yeates. Note the crude but effective handling equipment.

Before the construction of the Merchants' Railway, teams of up to 18 horses had to act as both motive and braking power over the steep roads of Underhill. John Upham's 1803 painting shows a cart passing cottages at Mallams, many of which still exist.

One landslip occurred in 1665 when the Great Pier, which had been built on the north-east side for the Banqueting House contract, was destroyed by a massive portion of cliff becoming detached and sliding into the sea. The pier was a platform of squared blocks projecting into the sea, and was the sole means by which stone was loaded, by a crude derrick type crane and jacks, into the barges. The following year a far greater disaster in London ironically brought salvation for Portland, for 1666 was the year of the Great Fire of London and the destruction of the old St Paul's Cathedral.

The nation's most celebrated architect, Christopher Wren, was engaged to design and supervise the rebuilding of the City of London and its cathedral following the Fire. As a young architect, Wren was already familiar with Portland Stone, so despite its high cost he insisted on using it for his greatest project, the new St Paul's Cathedral. The first stone was delivered to the St Paul's site in May 1676, and the contract tested both technology and ingenuity on the Island to the limits. There were times when the entire project was threatened, by disputes, accidents and even French pirates, but 35 years and six millions tons of Portland Stone later, St Paul's and some 50 London churches and other Wren buildings were completed, to be admired 300 years later by worshippers and visitors from all over the world.

As the quarries moved inland from the cliff edges it became increasingly difficult to dispose of the overburden and transport the stone. The grassy banks of the Weares between the cliffs and the shore had been important common land for sheep grazing. The Weares with their winding sheep-walks and lush growth then became valuable as rubble-dumping grounds. Time has mellowed these eighteenth and nineteenth centuries stone tips at the West and East Cliffs, so that they are now hard to distinguish from the natural cliff-fallen scree slopes. The undercliff Weares on both sides of the Island now provide the setting for a tranquil stroll – or an energetic ramble.

High on the side of Verne Hill is a popular footpath with massive stone blocks as a parapet, giving magnificent views over West Bay, This was the route of the Portland (or Merchants') Railway, which was a milestone for the stone industry. By 1824 some 27,000 tons of stone were being exported annually by sea from Portland. Getting it down to the shore was risky, inefficient – and cruel to the horses. That year fourteen stone merchants combined to promote a scheme for a railway from Tophill to the Castletown waterfront. They obtained an Act of Parliament to construct Dorset's first railway, a truly pioneering enterprise. When in 1825 Royal Assent was given for Portland's Merchants' Railway, it coincided with the opening of the somewhat more famous Stockton and Darlington Railway!

Teams of horses hauled stone carts on dirt roads from the quarries to the railway at Priory (the famous viewpoint on Portland Heights). There tolls were collected and the blocks were loaded by a timber derrick. From this point a narrow track passed around the steep

Opposite page top A truck being lowered on the steep incline to Castletown, on the historic Merchants Railway. Its descent was controlled by a cable passing around a braked wheel, the other end of which pulled up the empty wagons. The line closed in 1939.
Opposite page bottom Castletown Pier in the late nineteenth century, with a Cosens Weymouth-based paddle steamer on the right.

hillside in a gentle gradient, skirting the Verne's Great Common. Iron rails were fixed to stone sleepers, on which horses towed the flatbed trucks to the edge of a precipitous slope above the quay at Castletown. The trucks were then hitched to a chain running around a braked wheel and over rollers. Gravity did the rest, as the weight of laden trucks descending pulled the empty ones back up. This section is now known as the Merchants Incline. At the bottom horses again took over for the short journey to the jetties, where the stone was loaded onto barges. The Merchants' Railway operated for a remarkable 114 years, finally ceasing at the start of the Second World War.

In the late nineteenth century, stone saw mills and masonry yards were established, and Portlanders were now able to use their cutting and carving expertise on a larger scale. Steam power was readily adopted, both in saw mills and for motive power, and old hand derricks gradually gave way to steam cranes. Traction engines started to supersede horses for drawing stone in 1893. The metallic ring of flywheels, the clatter of gears and shrilling whistles; the smell of coal steam and the rutted roads became familiar to everyone on Portland until the late 1920s. Some of these iron monsters returned years later as brass-embellished showmen's engines driving whirligigs at Portland Fair.

Demand for Portland stone surged in late Victorian London. The chronicle of orders flowing to the Island begins to read like an architectural catalogue of the nation. Stone was produced and carved here for the huge London Law Courts. the Blackwall Tunnel, the Royal Exchange, countless banks, churches and railway stations, and for export to New York and China. At the turn of the century the Island supplied the Institution of Civil Engineers, Westminster, and Belfast City Hall (the finest stone building in Ireland, for which Portlander Jack Durston was Clerk of Works). Portland stone was used in the National Gallery, Tower Bridge, the Public Records Office in Chancery Lane, and many of the greatest façades in London, including the Admiralty Building in Whitehall. An all-time peak was reached in 1904 when Portland exported well over 100,000 tons of building stone.

After the near collapse of the industry in the Great War local firms managed to complete the contract for the County Hall, Westminster.

Traction engine FX 6661, better known as Kitchener , passing St John's
Church, Fortune's Well in 1921, on one of its five daily journeys to F.J.
Barnes stone yard by the railway station at Victoria Square.

In a corner of Wakeham opposite the Mermaid Inn, a stone plaque
by a group of stone cottages (built in 1997) now marks the site of the
little quarry opened exclusively for the great Whitehall Cenotaph
(1920). This was not the only tribute to those who died in the First
World War, as between 1919 and 1932 some half a million Common-
wealth War Grave stones and larger memorials were shipped from
Portland around the world.

Sheep were deprived of their pasture near Wakeham when stone
was taken to make Manchester's Midland Bank, Library and Ship
Canal Building, and for the restoration of Westminster Abbey in
1920. The ICI headquarters on Millbank began its life in a quarry
south of Weston in 1927. New inland quarries marched across the
beautiful fields of Broadcroft, Zilklake, Tombstone Acre, Shepherds

Dinner and Park Field (between Wakeham and the cliffs), providing a new façade for Regent Street and an extension to the British Museum to house the Elgin Marbles. The list could lengthen indefinitely. The Tate Gallery followed in 1935. Portland's quarriers worked closely with the foremost architects of the day on such buildings as the Daily Telegraph Building in Fleet Street, Broadcasting House in Portland Place, Cunard House, and the enormous University of London.

Stone for many of those buildings was carried across the Island by traction engines, and then by train, but by the time the last of the iron-wheeled steam road engines left in 1931 motor lorries were able to take on longer hauls. By then Portland had become the largest centre of stone masonry in the British Isles, if not Europe. Before the last war quarrymen were still paid 'tonnage money' for amounts of stone removed, and the four-man gangs, often of one family, were doubled with the advent of steam and electric cranes.

The task of rebuilding the country after the Second World War brought relative prosperity to the Portland stone industry. Once again the Island also had the task of supplying gravestones for the nation's war dead. By 1957 no less than 800,000 headstones and large memorials had been fashioned by Island masons and sent around the world. Vast quantities of masonry were turned out to rebuild the blitzed centres of Plymouth, Bristol, Southampton, Manchester, and London. Island masons surpassed themselves with their work for the National Library of Wales and the American Embassy. The biggest accolade for Portland Stone was the order to face part of the United Nations building in New York.

Ironically, the 'Island of Stone' even responded to the enthusiasm for concrete that swept the country in the 1950s and 1960s. At Wide Street, a huge masonry shed was adapted for a new venture, 'Portcrete', a form of 'reconstructed stone' made from waste rock. Perhaps its most famous product was London's towering Centre Point, for which every cruciform wall panel was precision-made on the Island and taken to the site by lorry. Portcrete duly closed, but traditional stone held its own. By 1965 the Bottomcombe masonry works at Easton was the largest in Europe, had the world's largest circular saw, and the latest electronically controlled machinery.

The late Skylark Durston (left), one of Portland's most famous sons, with fellow mason the late Doug Mitchell, working on a Corinthian capital for the National Gallery in 1973.

Demand for stone continued to grow, and in 1972 600 tons were donated for renovation work on St Paul's Cathedral. Among the blocks loaded onto a sailing barge at Castletown Pier was one originally selected and marked for Sir Christopher Wren, 300 years earlier: this is now displayed in the Cathedral crypt.

The Portland stone industry is an accurate thermometer of the nation's economic health, and suffers badly in any depression. However, with the approach of the twenty-first century the value of quality stone and traditional craftsmanship is once more being appreciated. The recent Sainsbury extension to the National Gallery is just one example of the exquisitely carved classical stonework now being produced on the Island.

The prosperity and pride that quarrying created is, and has always been, vital to each generation, but in many parts of Tophill all that remains of the historic pastoral landscape are the ancient field names. These names ill-fit the tracts of quarries and mounds of overburden often left when quarrying stops. But all is not lost, for where natural regeneration is encouraged, even recent quarries quickly turn green and become warm and sheltered habitats for Portland's precious flora and wildlife. These – along with geology and natural history trails – are key ingredients of one of the Island's main industries for the future – tourism.

ANCIENT DEFENCES

With its high cliffs, and being almost surrounded by sea, the Island enjoys superb natural defences against any invader. The Romans were not the first to recognise Portland's strategic importance. In about 400 BC Iron Age settlers threw up defences, including a high double embankment with lines of deep trenches around the west and south sides of Portland's high point, the grand Verne Hill. The summit of Verne Hill was not always the high flat hilltop we see today. In its original form, it was an even higher grassy dome commanding a 360° panorama of the Dorset coast and the English Channel.

The Iron Age Islanders also formed earth 'castles' at Southwell and near Blacknor Point, but these were insufficient to repel the Romans when they landed on Portland in about 60 AD. The Romans settled in some strength. Countless fragments from the Roman occupation have been found all over the Island, ranging from coins and pottery to hundreds of lidded stone sarcophagi, cut out of solid blocks of stone. The great hilltop camp at Verne Hill was strengthened in Romano-British times, making full use of the natural cliffs on its north and east sides, and a deep fissure to the south.

The Romans had fortified the Channel shores against Saxon raiders by the end of the third century AD. Although Saxons had conquered much of the country by 440, their domination of the area was not complete for another 200 years, since their strong defences provided commanding positions on Verne Hill, as well as similar vantage points elsewhere in Dorset. Once settled on Portland the Saxons laid down their weapons and developed new methods of working the land. It was they who established the Manor of Portland, with the King of Wessex, later of England, as its lord. They divided the land into fields, boundaries of which exist today, and had a more lasting impact on Portland's landscape and customs than any other settler.

Rufus Castle was built in about 1300 on the site of a Saxon defence, but despite its prominence much remains to be discovered about its building and early use.

The years of Saxon stability were violently shattered during the eighth century. Trading ships from continental Europe taking shelter in the lee of the island would have long been been a familiar sight, but the 80 feet longships seen approaching in the 8th century were the largest craft known on Portland since the departure of the Romans. Portland suffered one of the first Viking raids on the country, and was to endure their attacks for the next 200 years. Church Ope Cove may mark the site of their initial raid. From the east it was the only the natural beach on which to land, and the defenceless village of Wakeham was clearly visible from out to sea. But the Island was not easily conquered, for their adversaries enjoyed a fearsome reputation for slinging stones.

Following the successful 1065 invasion by the Normans, William the Conqueror took over all the land, dividing most of it amongst his supporters, but he retained the Manor of Portland for himself. Portland was the first entry in the Dorset section of the Domesday Book, indicating its strategic importance.

Portland's strategic position in the English Channel has always made it vulnerable to attack. With naval and commercial shipping expanding rapidly in the early sixteenth century, the sheltered waters of Portland Roads provided essential refuge from prevailing storm seas, but vessels were frequently attacked by French privateers.

Henry VIII's break from Catholicism, declared in 1531, raised the fear of invasion from France and Spain. To protect the anchorage between the Island and the mainland, two castles were constructed facing each other. Portland Castle, barely above sea level, was sited by the tidal inlet of the Mere, with its back to the massive Verne Hill. It cost precisely £4,964.19s.10d (equivalent to some £5m today), and when completed around 1539 was the most important 'place of arms' in Dorset. Its partner across the water at Weymouth was erected soon afterwards on a sandstone promontory, but from its earliest days Sandsfoot Castle suffered from sea erosion, and saw little action before becoming a ruin.

Portland Castle displays the impeccable work of the Tudor masons, who used stone brought down from the Island quarries. It was designed to resist the latest gunpowder ordnance of the day, with rounded walls to deflect artillery shot, and castellations and gun openings. But in practice the early soldiers still relied on the age-old bow and arrow. In its early years the Castle was also used to store some of the treasures taken from the Catholic convents.

Portland's vulnerability came into sharp focus when during the 1580's attention shifted to the marauding Spanish Armada. It was feared that 'the Spanish could land and the two castles could not reach them with a single shot'. The coastal beacons were prepared, and in 1588 one hundred extra soldiers with ordnance arrived to bolster the garrison. From the clifftops that year Portlanders were able to witness some of the most spectacular battles with the Spanish Armada, although these were out of sight of the Castle guns. The eventual defeat of the Armada did not end the scares of Spanish invasion.

Shipping movements in the Channel remained perilous, but nothing was done to keep the Castle in working order. Sir Walter Raleigh became Captain of Portland Castle in 1592, leaving his deputy in residence. The Castle's condition worsened. The timber roofing and flooring rotted, equipment became unserviceable. A wall had to be built to prevent the sea entering the moat, which actually contained fresh water, possibly for use in the Castle. A small rock breakwater was formed to stop the Castle being undermined by the sea, but little was done to preserve the building itself.

Portland Castle was one hundred years old before it saw its years of glory – it was the area's focal point in the Civil War (1642-1649). Being a fiercely Royal Manor, Portland naturally took King Charles' side. Despite being almost hopelessly under-manned and inadequately armed, the defenders managed to keep the Island out of Cromwellian hands for all but two periods of the war. The Castle was captured by Parliamentary 'Roundheads' in May 1643, only to be retaken for the king four months later.

For the next three years, Portland Castle fought off attack after attack. By 1645 only Portland, Corfe and Sherborne in the Wessex region remained held by Royalists. When defeat finally came in April 1646, Portland's surrender was bloodless, and on remarkably generous terms. But once entrenched here Cromwell's troops caused mayhem and destruction around the Island. The restoration of the monarchy in 1660 was therefore greeted with rejoicing on Portland,

Portland Castle in the nineteenth century.

and was marked with the placing of Charles II's coat of arms over a new outer gateway of the Castle.

By the start of the ninteenth century the old Castle was outdated and almost superfluous to defence needs, so in 1816 the keys were handed to the Portland Rector, Rev. John Manning, who moved in with his family. When John died in 1826, his 32 year-old son Charles was granted residency. Captain Charles Augustus Manning was to become perhaps the most powerful and influential Portland resident of the 19th century.

After his wife of only two years died in 1832, Manning lived alone and turned his attention, – and his wealth, enthusiasm and wood-working skills – to restoring and embellishing his Portland Castle home. He was Island governor in all but name, presiding over courts, inquiries and inquests, and he promoted prestigious hotel and hous-ing projects, including Victoria Square. Manning was in the forefront of the Breakwater scheme, having personally invited to HRH Prince Albert to perform the 1849 inauguration ceremony.

When Manning died in 1869 he left the Island a legacy of a lovingly restored Henrican castle, which otherwise would have decayed into an interesting but roofless ruin – or worse.

Back in War Office hands, Portland Castle did play minor military roles in the 20th century. In the Great War it was first an ordnance store and then accommodation for the embryonic Royal Naval Air Service. Year by year the Castle became enveloped by assortment of incongruous defence installations, and, with the filling of the old tidal Mere, its delightful setting was lost. In the Second World War Portland Castle hosted British and US military personnel, and it stood solidly by as tens of thousands of allied troops passed around it on D-Day 1944.

The Castle was first opened to the public in 1952, and was again restored when taken over as a National Heritage site in 1955.

Portland's story is full of ironies, and it is remarkable that Old Harry's little fort should shine and outlive all the great defence works of the 20th century, including the vast Royal Naval Air Station next door. The demise of the helicopter base gives an opportunity to once again give this priceless Ancient Monument a setting worthy of its place in English history.

THE HARBOUR AND BREAKWATER

The mass of Portland Island, together with Chesil Beach, protects a wide area of water – a superb anchorage which from ancient times has provided an excellent haven for shipping. Despite the shelter, Portland's coast has long been notorious for shipwrecks. For want of a refuge, a fleet of 200 merchant ships and military transports under Admiral Christian suffered catastrophic losses in a south-westerly storm near the Island in 1795. Only months earlier a local man, John Harvey, published the first proposal for building a Breakwater to form a proper harbour. Another half century was to pass before that dream became a reality.

The government was already debating how best to make use of Portland's natural harbour when Queen Victoria and her consort, Prince Albert, sailed into Portland Roads to a colourful welcome in 1843. The queen's sea-sickness prior to her arrival may not have

Queen Victoria and her consort Prince Albert arriving at Portland in 1843.

influenced the Royal Commission for Harbours of Refuge set up soon afterwards, but Prince Albert certainly played an influential role in the development of the Breakwater and the massive defence works needed to protect it.

The Commission was enthusiastic. Portland had the greatest strategic value of all the possible harbour sites it had considered. The potential for commercial shipping was already clear, but such were Portland's merits that it was decided to transform the Harbour into the first naval anchorage specifically designed for the new steam navy.

Prince Albert laid the first stone for the Royal Portland Breakwater in a grand ceremony on a July day in 1849. Its engineer, James Meadows Rendel, had developed a brilliant concept into firm plans, and work had already started on the vast infrastructure. Miles of railway and inclined planes were constructed to take the stone from the quarries on top of the Island down to the Breakwater site. It was a gargantuan task. The main contractor was John Towlerton Leather, a pioneer of technological innovation. Engineers, skilled craftsmen and administrators came from all parts of the country, while thousands of convicts who had been sentenced to transportation to the Colonies were brought here to hew the vast quantities of stone required. A large temporary Convict Establishment was built high above on Portland's East Cliff.

To construct the Breakwater Rendel designed a massive timber staging 37 metres wide supported on 33 metre-long piles screwed into the sea bed, guided into place by divers wearing primitive suits of leather, rubber and copper. The staging had to support five lines of railways, and the entire structure had to withstand storm conditions as it advanced two miles out into heaving seas. Visitors came from far and wide to view the progress as millions of tons of stone were laid. It was Victorian Dorset's greatest tourist attraction by far.

The scheme went on for the next quarter of a century, guided by Rendel's successor as Engineer-in-chief, Sir John Coode. He and John Leather were undaunted by the inevitable setbacks. A temporary wooden lighthouse was burnt down; the staging was torn asunder in storms; vessels were wrecked on the unfinished Breakwater wall; locomotives and trucks plunged into the sea, and lives were lost in terrible accidents. Despite the disasters the project was a

A section of the timber staging built to help construct the Breakwater.

success, and even before the first two arms were half completed the benefits to shipping were obvious.

In 1859 it was announced that because of the size of the new Harbour – already the largest man-made harbour in the world – Portland was to be the home port for Isambard Kingdom Brunel's immense steamship *Great Eastern* on its transatlantic passenger voyages. Fate determined otherwise when an explosion crippled the vessel before she arrived in 1860, and the legendary Brunel died whilst she was under repair at Portland. The *Great Eastern* proved unviable as a passenger liner, but returned to Portland several times during her successful undersea cable laying service.

If the Breakwaters themselves were of an awesome scale, the associated defence works were equally stupendous. Prince Albert made several visits to see the summit of the Verne Hill, overlooking the new harbour, being remoulded and transformed into the Verne Citadel. A smaller fort was constructed on Nothe Point, Weymouth, while a large fortress on the Breakwater posed the greatest engineering challenge of all. The importance of these works is illustrated by the fact that by the 1870s Portland had become the government's largest project, and was being constructed at a time when British pride and inspiration were at their peak following the Great

Exhibition of 1851. All these engineering works, and the gun batteries embedded in the Portland hillsides, were duly completed, and remain to this day monuments to Victorian boldness and ingenuity.

In 1862 *The Times* announced that the Training Ship *Britannia*, 'the nursery for our future admirals', was to be stationed at Portland. She stayed for three years, but was transferred to Dartmouth following its victory over Portland for the prestigious shore-based naval college. For forty years however, Portland Harbour was base for a succession of training ships, each named *Boscowen*.

The completion of the first two arms of the Breakwater was marked by an impressive ceremony in August 1872. Both the Channel and Reserve Squadrons, headed by a line of huge broadside ironclads, gave a royal salute to welcome the Prince of Wales. The inscription on the stone he laid includes the line '. . . These are Imperial Works and Worthy Kings'. These government works, which in one way or another involved the whole Island, and the presence of naval and military personnel, had an economic impact on the Island and South Dorset which was to last for 150 years.

The Harbour in late Victorian times was an impressive sight, with up to 200 head of sail at anchor or under way at any one time. The nation's – and the world's – largest vessels were regularly to be seen lying in the lee of the Breakwater, including the greatest of them all, HMS *Warrior*, Britain's first armour-plated battleship, which was fitted out with electric lighting while spending her semi-retirement years as Portland's guardship.

Development of the Harbour and Naval Base has continued without pause right to the end of the twentieth century. Two final Breakwater arms completed the enclosure of Portland Harbour in 1906, as a counter-measure against torpedo attack. Ironically, the torpedo was first developed at Whitehead's factory on the Wyke Regis frontage of the Harbour in the 1890s. This set the example for Portland's world pioneering research on underwater weapons through the ensuing century, from asdic and sonar in the 1920s to hi-tech Stingray torpedoes in the 1980s.

The early years of the century marked a period of rapid transition from coal and steam-powered vessels to oil. Costly coal handling machinery was now redundant, and a prime wildlife habitat – an ancient tidal creek called the Mere – in the south-west corner of the Harbour, was turned into a fuel tank farm, whose vast cylinders still dominate the approach to Portland.

The looming conflict with Germany before the Great War saw the arrival of the Dreadnoughts, whilst the sound of propellers in the skies overhead announced the arrival of the first aeroplanes. King George V watched aerial displays from the royal yacht in the Harbour in 1912, an occasion marked by the first ever flight from a moving ship and the first royal trip in a submarine. Two years later the Grand Fleet assembled in Portland Harbour before sailing to Scapa Flow, leaving behind the old battleship HMS *Hood*, which was scuttled to block the vulnerable South Ship Channel between the first two Breakwater arms.

The peace of the 1920s turned to anxiety in the 1930s with the realisation that a second World War was inevitable. In 1936 Edward VIII came to see for himself Portland's top secret research and to watch naval manoeuvres. The preparations were not in vain, as the Harbour was to play a vital role in the Second World War. Among many terrifying episodes was the bombing of the anti-aircraft ship *Foylebank* when stationed in the Harbour in July 1940. Crewman Jack Mantle was mortally wounded but valiantly stayed at his post firing at the enemy raiders until he fell, for which he was awarded the Victoria Cross.

Portland's war culminated in the greatest assembly of men and machines this coast has ever seen. In 1944 enormous Mulberry Harbour 'Bombardon' units were towed into Portland ready to be taken across the Channel. On 1st May the base was commissioned as USNAAB *Portland-Weymouth*. When George VI, Winston Churchill and General De Gaulle arrived to inspect the D-Day preparations the entire harbour was awash with landing craft, troop transporters and their naval escorts. Between D-Day itself and the end of the war nearly half-a-million men and 144,000 vehicles were embarked from either Portland or Weymouth. Portland's contribution was noted by messages from the United States: '. . . for over a year your Island of Portland has been a key factor in the movement of troops and their weapons of war to the far shore in the liberation of the Continent . . .;' 'you are the biggest little port in the world, you have been wonderful.' The Island's contribution to Operation Overlord was commemorated in 1945 when the American ambassador unveiled a plaque in Victoria Gardens.

Post-war peace brought many changes. Ships of NATO nations began to frequent the Harbour as the Naval Base adapted to its role as the prime work-up and training centre. A new dimension was added in 1959 with the formation of a naval helicopter base, for which the last vestiges of the old Mere creek were filled in to provide the largest helicopter airfield in Europe. HMS *Osprey*'s helicopter squadrons have been at the forefront of many incidents around the globe, while in recent years its Search and Rescue service (now a Coastguard operation) has saved countless lives around Dorset's coast and beyond.

Any belief that the expenditure of £25 million on building naval accommodation blocks at Castletown in 1985 would secure the Royal Navy's presence at Portland was dispelled when it was announced in

Portland Harbour after the Second World War, when it was still a major work-up base for navies of the NATO countries.

A small flotilla returns to harbour in July 1995 having honoured the
departure of Portland's last Flag Officer Sea Training. The White ensign on
the right is being lowered for the last time. The great East Weares Batteries
and Fort await discovery by the next generation of tourists.

1993 that the historic Portland Naval Base was to close, due to the
ending of the Cold War. The departure of the last Flag Officer Sea
Training in 1995 terminated a long and proud era for the Island.
With the last helicopters due to depart from the Royal Naval Air
Station in 1999, Portland will be left with no formal military
presence for the first time in more than 500 years.

The island is now seeing the reincarnation of Portland Harbour
into a more peaceful but still animated scene. Commerce, shipping,
fishing and recreational activities are all playing a part. Portland
Royal Naval Base is now Portland Port. The first years of private
enterprise have transformed the Harbour faster than many had dared
hoped. The huge old coaling pier, alongside which there are berths
for some of the largest vessels afloat, has been reconstructed to house
the maritime division of the giant Cable and Wireless company.
Cruise ships call; the old HMS *Osprey* complex at East Weares is
being converted into a holiday village; and a multitude of commercial and tourism-related ventures are growing.

THE VERNE CITADEL

Nothing on the Island has had so permanent an impact on the historically insular Portland community as the building of the Verne Citadel and its associated defences. Its primary purpose was to house troops to man the shore defences, and protect ships at anchor from within its fortified barracks and siege fort. The Citadel itself occupies 56 acres, but twice this area of surrounding land was completely remoulded to form defensible slopes called 'glacis'. The form of the Verne Ditch and ramparts was taken from the ancient earthworks, but all signs of the latter were lost when the 'ditch' – really a vast dry moat – was quarried out to provide stone for the Breakwaters. The Royal Engineers took a leading role in the planning and construction of the Verne Citadel, and the East Weares and High Angle Batteries nearby. The project took thirty years to complete. Convicts did most of the manual labour (it was the largest job ever done by British prisoners), and the skilled work was by civilian contractors.

Prince Albert made frequent visits to the site. His final inspection was in August 1861, just four months before his death, when the first 50 casemated barracks fronting the parade ground were being completed. Above the casemates are high earth ramparts, which conceal the barracks behind, so that from a distance all that can be seen are geometric grass banks. Heavy guns were mounted on the cliff tops on the east side, and overlooking West Bay to fire at any enemy landing on Chesil Beach.

The Verne could accommodate 3000 men. Everything was on a monumental scale. There was a hospital, gymnasium, recreation rooms, canteens, museum, tennis and squash courts, even a cricket ground, all invisible from land or sea in the recessed hilltop. Water storage was by an ingenious underground system which provided a capacity of 430,000 gallons of rainwater, supplemented by a piped supply from a steam pumping station three miles away at Southwell.

The Great Verne Ditch was dug by convicts, Royal Engineers, and civilian contractors. In the 1860's and 1870's millions of tons of stone were taken by steam and gravity railways down to the Breakwater works.

The Royal Engineers supervised the building of zig-zag roads up the steep terrain from Fortune's Well and through the wild East Weares. One million tons of stone were taken from the ditch, which is 37 metres wide and 22 metres deep. It was transported by a specially constructed steam railway around the north-eastern clifftop and via a rope-controlled Incline Railway down to the Breakwater. There were magnificent sallyports on the south-eastern and south-western sides, the latter having a drawbridge over the ditch. The Great South Gate was designed in 1874; defended by caponiers and a dropping drawbridge spanning the moat. The Great North Gate is

The sheer size and scale of the Verne engineering works is difficult to comprehend. The entire hilltop and sides were reshaped to form one of Victorian Britain's greatest defences.

equally spectacular. Its long arched tunnel is completed by a portcullis and underground guard rooms, whilst a now-public viewpoint nearby commands a fine panoramic view of Weymouth and the South Dorset coastline.

THE CONVICTS

Dominating the clifftop at Grove Point is a large complex of multi-storey institutional blocks. The once white Portland stone walls of these enormous buildings have become silvery grey with a century of weathering. They now house some of the country's Young Offenders, successors to the Borstal Boys who first came here in 1921. It is ironic that the generally law-abiding Portlanders, who neither had nor needed any prison of their own, should for the last century and a half have played host to countless 'Kimberlin' criminals ('Kimberlin' is the old Portland name for anyone not born and bred on the Island).

The government's realization that the scale of the nineteenth century Breakwaters, together with the forts, gun batteries and other defences, was too massive for civilian or military labour inspired its decision to use convicts. From 1848 convicts were brought to the Island by the thousand to quarry and work the millions of tons of stone required. The spectacle of the pioneer convicts being marched over Verne Hill to the clifftop site alarmed Islanders traditionally slightly suspicious of any strangers. As it turned out, discipline was so strict that Island life was affected more by the hoards of civilians and soldiers who came than by the convicts. For some it proved a blessing. All the convicts arriving here had been sentenced to transportation in the colonies. The arrangement was that by hard work and good behaviour at Portland, they could earn a 'ticket of leave' to reduce their sentence, or even a conditional discharge, after they arrived at their destination abroad.

The first convicts to arrive had to help build their own prison at the Grove – huge temporary structures of tin and timber. A high stone wall was built around the complex, which comprised four large halls with 700 cells, separated by corrugated iron partitions. In a space just seven feet long and four feet wide each inmate had a

The Grove – an anciently mysterious area overlooking East Cliff – was the site chosen for the huge temporary prison of 1848. It originally housed up to 1500 convicts brought to quarry stone for the Breakwater, but became a permanent establishment in 1869.

hammock, stool, and table. The infrastructure needed to make the establishment function was immense. Roads, drainage, gasworks, a reservoir, chapel, baths, canteens, laundry, blacksmiths and masonry shops were all constructed. The convicts required guarding, both by well-armed warders and by military detachments.

Life for the convicts was hard. Fatal accidents occurred in the frantic effort to feed the gigantic Breakwater works with stone. The prisoners worked with pickaxes and barrows for ten hours a day, first clearing the soil from hundreds of acres of historic fields, then removing the overburden down to the stone beds, many metres below the original surface. With some foresight a large pillar of rock was left unquarried, which enables us to see how much ground was removed. This stack, known as Nichodemus' Knob (after an older land feature nearby) is on the edge of the cliff just south of the Verne Citadel. In the course of these operations, between the Grove and Verne Yeates, countless remnants from earlier ages and civilisations – fossils, tools, burials, standing stones and monoliths – were found, briefly noted – and discarded.

Once exposed the stone was cut away in large blocks, roughly squared, and lifted onto trucks. Pieces that were to be worked were taken to masonry workshops in the prison, while the bulk stone for the Breakwaters was conveyed directly down the cliffside on an incline railway system to supply the huge mound advancing into the open sea. By 1851 825 convicts were at work in the quarries, but within four years the number had reached nearly 2,000. There was terrible overcrowding and the prison had to be extended. Escapes were rare, but attempts were frequent and often ingenious – including scaling the steep cliffs down to homemade rafts. Although troops were permanently quartered near the prison, a telegraph line was set up between the Grove and Weymouth Barracks after mass-escapes and a mutiny were attempted. The regime was harsh and in 1897 the Director of Prisons conceded that, 'The punishments inflicted at Portland far exceed those at any other convict prison, both in number and severity' – in fact twice as many as at Dartmoor. It was not

Convicts sentenced to Transportation were brought to Portland to quarry stone for the Breakwater. By hard work and good conduct they could earn a measure of freedom when they arrived at Australia or the other colonies.

much easier for the warders, who were instantly dismissed if any convict in their charge escaped. At least two were murdered on duty, and those who were found trafficking tobacco with prisoners were punished with up to six months hard labour.

Among the hard, toughened criminals were cases of sadness and tragedy, and mothers and wives came to wave final farewells to loved ones departing on the convict ships from Castletown for the colonies. It is a mistake to think of all those convicts as hardened thugs. Some certainly were, but amongst their ranks were victims of deprivation who had resorted to stealing bread or a few coins to feed their families. Prejudice was more common than compassion; seven years hard labour and transportation for stealing a shilling or two was not unusual.

The prison was intended to be temporary, for the duration of the Breakwater scheme. Portlanders hoped that the ending of transportation as a punishment in 1868 would lead to the prison's closure, so anger greeted the announcement a year later that the prison was to be made permanent. A petition was raised in an attempt to persuade the government to change its mind, but to no avail. Enterprising Islanders soon exploited the situation. Victorian and Edwardian tourists came from all over the country to see the convicts at work. Good livings were made by providing ponies and traps for guided tours. Morbidly curious visitors were taken to some cottages in Grove Road which had upstairs tea rooms, from where they could peer over the walls of the convict quarries.

The large stone buildings which can now be seen from all over Tophill were erected in the 1890s, in traditional form – long high central halls with metal balconies and galleries of cells along each side. The stonework on the monumental façades is of a high quality, and the entire complex is now a Conservation Area. Pride was evident in the carefully tended Governor's gardens, and in much other work of the prisoners in the area. The best example of the convicts' skills is to be seen in St Peter's Church at Grove Road. The church was planned when the convicts' work for the original Breakwaters was nearing completion, and both were finished in the same year, 1872. It was also the garrison church for the soldiers stationed at the Verne, and a tablet inside lists the many regiments who served in

St Peter's Church was built in 1872 by convicts as the garrison church for the military regiments stationed at the Verne Citadel.

the Citadel. St Peter's was built in the grand Romanesque style, and despite the 'free' labour it was the most expensive church ever erected on the Island. Inside, the reason for the cost is clear: the magnificent open-timbered roof, carved pews, and intriguing mosaic flooring – the work of female prisoners (in jails elsewhere) supervised by Constance Kent, who as a young girl was convicted and condemned by her confession to the murder of her four-year-old stepbrother: it now seems that Constance was innocent, and only admitted to the crime to protect her father and his mistress.

The last of the old-style convicts, who included Irish Fenians and Conscientious Objectors, finally departed after the First World War. Once again there was a prospect of Portland being free of the association with criminal institutions. However in 1921 it was announced that the Portland prison buildings were to be used as one of the new Borstal Institutes. The younger inmates never produced public works to match St Peter's, but in the 1930s they did transform an old deep quarry into a superb Wembley-sized oval stadium.

To the north of the Grove, the Verne Citadel was finally declared redundant for military use after the Second World War. Fate could have transformed this magnificent hilltop site into one on the country's finest themed tourist attractions, but this was not to be. In 1949 the government decided that the vast complex would make an ideal training establishment – for prisoners. So HM Verne Prison was established. Conversion and building work over the first thirty years destroyed some of the Victorian features, but the great ditch, earthworks, tunnels, and casemates that survive are now protected as a scheduled Ancient Monument.

1996 saw the defensible nature of Portland again being put to use, for an innovation which attracted world-wide interest. An accommodation vessel, a veteran of the Falklands War, was towed to Portland Harbour to become the temporary prison ship HMP *Weare*. It remains to be seen whether this will be as temporary as the the 1848 establishment at the Grove!

THE RAILWAYS

Portland was connected to the main line railway network for exactly one hundred years. The branch line from Weymouth to Portland was opened in 1865, just thirty-six years after the building of the Ferry Bridge provided the Island with its first road link with the world beyond.

However the story of railways on Portland begins much earlier. Visiting the Island in 1804, the Reverend J. Skinner remarked on the cruel way horses were used to haul the heavy stone blocks down to the piers on crude brakeless carts. 'All this labour', he wrote, 'might easily be obviated by the simple construction of a railroad. Why this has not been long since performed is to me surprising, especially as Portland stone is in universal request.' The seed was sown, leading in 1825 to the decision to construct the Merchants' Railway from near the quarries at Priory to the waterfront at Castletown.

That same year a plan was put to the Admiralty for a similar but larger three-stage inclined railway system over East Cliff and down the steep banks of Weares to take stone to the Breakwater, then being planned. Work on the incline tramway, and other lines within the port area, started in 1847, and four years later the system was fully operational as the Admiralty Breakwater Railway. The Breakwater's contractor, John Leather, brought the· first steam locomotive to Portland that same year. The engineers had the foresight to build the new railways to broad gauge (7ft ¼in.) even though there was to be no link to the mainland for another thirteen years. The lines leading to the top of the Admiralty Incline were extended to the Verne hilltop, via a precarious cliff ledge overlooking the harbour, through a short tunnel and into the cavernous dry moat of Verne Ditch. Another line carried heavily laden stone trucks over high temporary wooden bridges back to the Grove. Small steam engines hauled these trains, but in the civilian quarries horses were generally used on a sinuous network of lines laid across Tophill from the 1850s.

With the arrival of the main line railway to Weymouth in 1857, an extension to Portland allowing easier access to the Breakwater works became inevitable. Five years later the Weymouth & Portland Railway Company was formed. Soon tunnels, bridges, cuttings and embankments were under construction on the Weymouth side as track was laid to the low causeway alongside Chesil Beach, the last major structure being a timber viaduct over the tidal entrance at Smallmouth. The line terminated at Chiswell, where Portland Station filled the fourth side of the new Victoria Square.

The line had to provide both Great Western Railway's broad gauge and the LSWR's narrow gauge, as both companies alternately operated the line. In practice only narrow gauge trains were used. The battle of the gauges was ended in 1874 when Brunel's vision for a wide gauge to be the universal standard was finally lost. On Portland, as elsewhere, the third rail was then removed.

On the morning of May 25th 1865 Islanders watched the locomotive 'Clyde', hauling a single carriage, a van and a horse box, steam slowly into Portland Station, carrying top-hatted officials from the two operating companies. The first ever passenger train on the island followed that October – six small four-wheeled coaches hauled by the 'Nile' – and a public dinner was held at the Royal Victoria Hotel, Chiswell, to celebrate the opening of the line.

The line quickly developed, enabling businesses – especially the stone companies – to expand. It revolutionised mail and packet services for Portlanders, and gave young people opportunities for travel undreamt of by their parents. Chesil fishermen were able to send their catches to distant markets for better prices. The traffic was two way, as Victorian tourists arrived to marvel at everything this unusual Island had to offer, including the great government works, the convicts, Chesil Beach, and the fossil-strewn quarries.

The public railway initially ended at Chiswell, but a branch line was immediately constructed, curving along the shore of the Mere, under a new bridge at Castle Road, to the foot of the old Merchants' Railway Incline at Castletown. This allowed stone from the top of the Island, which previously could only be exported by sea, to be

Portland Station terminus viewed from Chesil Beach. The opening of the railway link to the mainland in 1865 was a momentous event. It transformed the economy of Portland, and opened up a new world for many Islanders.

carried by rail. Unfortunately the gauge of the horse-and gravity-operated Merchants' Railway was different to the public line, and so a gantry transfer siding had to be built there. Not all stone took this route, some was brought to the Station down the steep hillside through Fortune's Well by cart, and later by traction engines, whilst much continued to go by sea barges from the Stone Pier at Castletown.

This arrangement, while infinitely better than before the railway, involved costly triple handling. What was needed was a rail link to the heart of the quarries on the top of the Island, but the escarpment of Underhill was an impossible obstacle. The only practicable route was a long circuit around the East Weares, up to the high cliffs above Church Ope Cove. This seemed too ambitious at the time, and so the Easton & Church Hope Railway was formed in 1867 to build a totally isolated railway from Easton to a proposed shipping pier at Church Ope Cove. Construction from Easton reached the cliff top

The railway around the East Cliffs to Easton was one of the most scenic coastal lines in the country. It was laid to the maximum possible gradient and was prone to rock falls and landslides. The last train ran on it in 1965.

near Pennsylvania before the scheme was abandoned. The locals were not surprised. Below the cliff lay the Southwell Landslip, one of the most unstable slopes on the island.

The Easton and Church Hope Railway was resurrected in the 1880's for a more conventional scheme; extending the Castletown and Breakwater lines to Easton (with sub branches to Weston village, and to Priory Corner at the top of the Island, neither of which were pursued). The Castletown branch had already (1878) been linked up to the Admiralty's Breakwater Railway, once landslips there had been stabilised. Further around the coast, the problem of constructing a railway over the notoriously unstable Kimmeridge clay slopes of East Weares was formidable, and it took ten years of planning before work could start. The task of laying the line to Easton, with its ten bridges, viaduct, and cutting through the sheer cliff face, took another decade. Under the high Yelland Cliffs a wire was strung along the trackside which would set signals to red if moved by rockfalls. This occasionally happened, and the line was closed several times, notably in 1907 when a huge fall took a long section of track down the hillside.

A piece of land called Lady Mead, near the centre of the village, was acquired for the Easton terminus. The delightful Easton Station opened at the dawn of the Edwardian era in 1902. It was built in a sheltered cutting, and had separate general and 'Ladies' waiting rooms. Unfortunately it had to be rebuilt after a disastrous fire only a year later, but successive station masters took pride in their colourful flower beds and fossil displays along the single platform.

Down at Chiswell the branch line to Easton veered off before the

Easton Station in 1906, with its engine shed and water tower on the right. The site is now occupied by Lady Mead Hall.

original terminus in Victoria Square, and so a new station had to be built on the curve by the Mere. It was raised on timber piles to allow floodwaters to flow to the Harbour, as seepage and overtopping of Chesil Beach was frequent. The new station was opened in 1905, ending complaints about the 'deathtrap' platform at the old terminus building, which later was converted into a goods depot.

The line was extremely busy during the Great War, conveying troops stationed at Verne Citadel, sailors to the port, and supplies to the giant Whitehead's Torpedo Factory at Wyke Regis. By the early 1930s new, cheaper, bus services began to take passengers away from the railway. The Easton and Church Hope Railway, which had actually been in receivership since 1908, was now losing £1500 a year. At the same time the stone firms were quick to acquire newly developed motor lorries capable of transporting stone more directly to their destinations.

The Second World War was nearly the end of private company control of the Portland line. The Island, with its strategic naval base, was a prime target for the enemy, and the railway took no less than 13 direct hits in bombing raids. After a brief return to civilian control after the war, the line was taken over by the nationalised British Railways in 1948. By then other forms of transport were available. Buses were frequent and cheap. Car ownership was increasingly common. British Railways decided to close the line to passenger service, running the last regular train on March 3rd 1952. The track was maintained for another thirteen years for goods traffic. The end finally came in 1965 when the last 'specials' carried enthusiasts, with many local people experiencing a ride on their own line for the first and last time.

The rails remained in place until 1971 while the Admiralty pondered the railway's strategic value. Since then the bridges, viaducts and other structures have been removed. Parts of the line have been built over, or absorbed into adjoining development, and the most impressive part of the route is now a footpath. Walkers exploring under the cliffs from above Church Ope around to East Weares can now both enjoy the magnificent panoramic seascape, and wonder why a previous generation lacked the vision to exploit the potential of one of the most scenic coastal branch lines in the country.

FURTHER READING

Betty, J.H., *The Island & Royal Manor of Portland, 1750-1851*, 1970
Bayley, A.R., *The Great Civil War in Dorset*, 1910
Attwooll, Maureen and West, Jack, *Weymouth, An Illustrated History*, 1983
Attwooll, Maureen and Harrison, Denise, *Weymouth & Portland at War*, 1993
Burnett, David, *Dorset Before The Camera*, 1982
Carter, Geoffrey, *The Royal Navy at Portland Since 1845*, 1987
Ching, Mark, and Currie, Ian, *The Dorset Weather Book*, 1997
Damon, Robert, *Geology of Weymouth & Portland*, 1884
Dyson, Peter, *A Century of Cinema in Dorset*, 1996
Edwards, Jean and Legg, Rodney, *Old Portland*, 1983
Guttridge, Roger, *Dorset Smugglers*, 1984
Jackson, Brian, *The Railways of Portland*, 1997
Morris, Stuart, *Portland, An Illustrated History*, 1985
    Portland Camera, 1990
    Portland in Old Picture Postcards, 1983
    Portland Pocket Guide, 1984
Palmer, Susann, *Mesolithic Cultures in Britain*, 1977
Ricketts, Eric, *The Buildings of Old Portland*, 1979
Warren, J.W., *The Royal Manor of Portland*, 1939
Wollage, Robert, series of Portland booklets including *Soft Burr & Whitbed*

The

DISCOVER DORSET

Series of Books

A series of paperback books providing informative illustrated
introductions to Dorset's history, culture and way of life.
The following titles have so far been published.

BRIDGES *David McFetrich and Jo Parsons*

CASTLES AND FORTS *Colin Pomeroy*

CRANBORNE CHASE *Desmond Hawkins*

GEOLOGY *Paul Ensom*

THE GEORGIANS *Jo Draper*

THE INDUSTRIAL PAST *Peter Stanier*

ISLE OF PURBECK *Paul Hyland*

LEGENDS *Jeremy Harte*

PORTLAND *Stuart Morris*

POTTERY *Penny Copland-Griffiths*

THE PREHISTORIC AGE *Bill Putnam*

SAXONS AND VIKINGS *David Hinton*

SHIPWRECKS *Maureen Attwooll*

STONE QUARRYING *Jo Thomas*

THE VICTORIANS *Jude James*

All the books about Dorset published by The Dovecote Press
are available in bookshops throughout the county,
or in case of difficulty direct from the publishers.
The Dovecote Press Ltd, Stanbridge,
Wimborne, Dorset BH21 4JD
Tel: 01258 840549.